How to Get on Radio Talk Shows All Across America

Without Leaving Your Home or Office

Joe Sabah

Pacesetter Publications

Other books by Joe Sabah

Co-authored with Judy Sabah
How to Get the Job You Really Want
and Get Employees to Call You

Printed in the United States of America

ISBN # 978-0-940923-12-6
Cover and interior design by Karen Saunders

Joe Sabah
Pacesetter Publications
P O Box 101330
Denver CO 80250
303-722-7200
Email: Joe@JoeSabah.com
www.JoeSabah.com

Dedicated to the loving memories of
my sister Louise, and brothers John and Frank
You paved the way. You taught me well.

A Special Thank You
to those who helped
make this book possible. . . .
Judy Sabah
(My #1 Angel)
Margie Schutte
Diana Hall

About the Author

Joe Sabah, Author, Speaker & Publisher provides proven, creative/innovative ideas to help you sell more books, CDs, DVDs, newsletters or your ideas without leaving your home or office.

He is co-author of the book: *How to Get the Job You Really Want and Get Employers to Call You.*

Joe has been a guest on over 723 Radio Talk Shows all across America. His results so far: 23,750 books sold . . . all at FULL RETAIL. That's more than $376,000 worth of books.

He has spoken to 18 state and regional associations of both speakers and publishers on *How to Create Book and Speech Titles that Sizzle and Sell* and *How to Get On Radio Talk Shows All Across America Without Leaving Your Home or Office.*

A member of NSA (National Speakers Association) since 1980, Joe was the founding president of CSA (Colorado Speakers Association). He was honored with a Life Membership.

Joe served CIPA (Colorado Independent Publishers Association), as president for 2 1/2 years. Joe was named a Life Member in 2003.

Table of Contents

Chapter 1

Picture This Scenario

Phone rings.

Joe: "Good Morning. This is Joe Sabah. How may I help you?"

Radio Talk Show Producer: "Good Morning, Joe. This is Charlie Talk Show Producer with WXYZ. I have Sally Talk Show Host waiting on the line for your interview. Are you ready?"

Joe: "Yes I am, Charlie. How long will I be on the air with Sally?"

Charlie: "About 30 minutes minus commercials."

Joe: "Will she have listeners calling in?"

Charlie: "Most likely. Hold on please. We're just 30 seconds away from air time."

Joe: "Thanks, Charlie."

Fade in

★ ★ ★ On The Air ★ ★ ★

Sally Radio Talk Show Hostess: "And now radio station WXYZ welcomes our special guest Joe Sabah. He joins us this morning by telephone from Denver, Colorado.

Joe co-authored the book, *How to Get the Job You Really Want and Get Employers to Call You.* Good Morning, Joe and welcome to station WXYZ's Morning Talk with Sally."

Joe: "Good Morning, Sally. It's my pleasure to be with you and your listeners.

Sally: "Joe, your book has a most intriguing title, especially with the promise to our listeners that they can have employers calling them. Would you tell us how you came up with this idea and how our listeners can use these job getting techniques?"

Joe: "I'd be delighted to Sally. Back in 1979 my son Joe had just graduated from high school and asked me to help him get a job. The only problem? Joe lives in Concord, California — I live in Denver, Colorado — 1,200 miles apart. So I created the first . . ."

★ ★ ★ 28 minutes and several callers later ★ ★ ★

Sally: "Joe our last half hour has just flown by. Thank you for covering so many good ideas in such a short time, especially the three tips on how a person can turn every job interview into a job offer. Our listening audience and the people who called in will be able to use your ideas to help them get the job they really want.

"One last question: How can our listeners of WXYZ get a copy of your book, *How to Get the Job You Really Want and Get Employers to Call You?"*

Joe: "Since our book is not in all the book stores, we have a website your listeners can use to order the book today. The book is entitled *How to Get the Job You Really Want and Get Employers to Call You."* Your jobs book will be sent to you via US Priority Mail. All for only $19.95, when you go to www.JoeSabah.com. And you will get an immediate download of the E-Book!"

The jobs book will be sent out the same day the call is received. The website again is: **www.JoeSabah.com."**

Sally: "Thanks again, Joe. I am looking forward to having you back again soon."

Joe: "Thanks, Sally. I'll do that. And thank you for a very professional interview. I look forward to being back with you again also. Please thank Charlie (producer) for getting us together."

★ ★ ★ ★ ★ ★

A dream?

No. This scenario has been repeated over 723 times.

As a result, I have sold over 22,750 copies of my book all at the retail price of $19.95. That's more than $376,000 in book sales . . . all at FULL RETAIL.

Kaching!

Averaging $534 per show, netting $454 per show.

Follow the steps outlined in the following chapters and . . .

This same thing can be happening to you, too.

You can be on the road to accomplishing the same . . . OR MORE!

Let's get started . . . NOW!

Chapter 2

Two Ideas That Started It All

Why would you want to be on Radio Talk Shows?

- ★ You love to talk
- ★ You have something to say to the world
- ★ You want more publicity
- ★ You want to increase your exposure
- ★ You have a book, CD, DVD or Tip sheet to offer
- ★ You want to increase your sales and profits

There are all these reasons and more for you to want to be interviewed on talk radio.

Here's how it all started for me . . .

Have you ever had a good idea, maybe even a "great" idea and wondered how to tell the rest of the world about it?

Back in 1979 I had **Idea #1** (a Job Getting System that I used to help my son Joe get a job — even though we were 1,200 miles apart). This idea became a seminar and ultimately a book: *How to Get the Job You Really Want and Get Employers to Call You.*

Next, it took me from 1979 to 1987 to find the right answer to: "How can I tell the rest of the world about my success formula for helping other people find their right employment?"

Idea #2 involved my decision to promote the book via Radio Talk Shows. This idea created the scenario described in Chapter One. In this book you will discover how I was able to sell over 22,750 copies of my book. With this formula and the list of radio stations, you too can do the same thing **or more.**

Back to **Idea #1:**

When my son Joe graduated from high school, I wanted to help him even though I was 1,200 miles away. So rather than just say "Congratulations!" I asked him: "What can I get you for graduation, son?"

He didn't hesitate . . . "Help me get a job, Dad!"

So I asked Joe what kind of job he wanted, and he told me that he wanted to be a printer. He described in detail the types of presses and cameras he operated at his part-time job. He enjoyed the work and now wanted to work full-time.

So I said, "Joe, I have an idea. Let me put it together and I'll call you back."

I thought about all the skills and talents I had used so far: recruiting sales agents for a large life insurance company, promoting speakers nationally, and selling salespeople and managers on attending motivational events.

I decided to draw on everything in my background to help my son. I put together the first Gold Form and called Joe back and read the following to him:

AVAILABLE IMMEDIATELY . . . .

One Qualified, Experienced, Responsible, Dependable
Printer I have run the following equipment:
- ★ A. B. Dick 360
- ★ A. B. Dick 360CD
- ★ A. B. Dick 385
- ★ Multi 1250

    Folders, several makes and models

    Agfa Gaevert Repromaster Camera

    Cutters, both electric and hand

    A. B. Dick 133 Platemaker

    A. B. Dick 675 Platemaker

Besides graduating from graphic classes in high school, I work
2-1/2 days per week in an in-house print shop.

My reason for leaving is to secure FULL-TIME employment.
(My present employer knows of my desires, but has need for only
a part-time person.)

I am 6 feet, 165 lbs., and in excellent health.

I will be 18 in January and have graduated from high school.

Your Company Will Gain:
- ★ An experienced printer
- ★ A dependable person who wants to work
- ★ A responsible individual who will put out work that will
- ★ bring in repeat orders
- ★ Cut down on turnover as I'm looking for a permanent position

Help Solve Your Printer Problems Today.

Call 925-xxx-xxxx and ask for Joe Sabah
I live at 1234 Willow Lane, Concord, CA 94520

AND I'M AVAILABLE IMMEDIATELY. . . . .

My conversation with my son took place on a Wednesday evening. The next morning I took this form to a quick print shop. I asked the lady at the counter if she would print 37 copies of this form.

(I chose 37 because that's the number of print shops in the yellow pages for Contra Costa County California where my son lives.)

She asked me the **most important question I've ever been asked:**

"What color paper do you want it on?"

With my corporate and resume mindset, I was thinking "white, buff, ivory." Then I asked her, "What is the **brightest** color you have?"

She responded with, "Goldenrod."

(For more details on, **"Why Goldenrod May Be a Stroke of Genius,"** please refer to Chapter 10.)

I said, "Let's go with it!" I was daring enough to experiment with something new. I must have been thinking, "What the heck. It's only $5.55 worth of postage."

On Thursday afternoon I mailed out 37 copies of the very **first** "Gold Form."

The following Tuesday (3 business days later) Joe called with the good news. "Guess what Dad. I got three job offers! And **they called me!**"

Boy, was Joe excited! Boy, was I excited! Just knowing that I was helping my son get his perfect job (with 1,200 miles between us) made me proud and excited. What better graduation gift could I give one of my three children? The gift of knowing that he will always be able to get a job anytime he wants . . . just by using the Gold Form.

Next I wondered, "How could I help other people use this Gold Form idea?"

I let my idea simmer for a while. To test this concept further I expanded on the job-getting idea by offering a seminar entitled, *How to Get the Job You Want.* I presented this program through community colleges and adult education programs throughout the Denver Metro area.

Ultimately I expanded the seminar and re-titled it, *How to Get the Job You Really Want and Get Employers to Call You.* This seminar was filled to capacity every single term during the nine years it was offered.

The "Gold Form" and the seminar comprise the first idea that worked out well for the first nine years. Hardly a month went by without several people asking: "How can people in other cities get this valuable information?"

I'd reply, "Some day I plan to take it nationally."

The "someday" finally happened when the seminar was put into book form, but the book was only available in the Denver Metro area.

Then came **Idea #2.**

In August 1986, a friend called and asked me if I would be available to be a guest on his local radio talk show.

This was not new to me. I had previously appeared as a guest on several talk shows. I said yes. During that interview I mentioned my book several times. The radio station's phone started ringing while I was still on the air. The question most often asked from callers was: "Where is the book available?"

Not knowing what else to say, I gave the listeners my home and office phone number. By the time I arrived home there were 12 calls on my recorder, ALL of them orders.

THAT was the beginning of **Idea #2.**

I discovered that listeners of radio talk shows want "more" of what talk show guests have to offer. They **expect** talk show guests to be published authors, or at least have something else to offer that the listeners can order.

Idea #2 took several months to germinate.

It actually took hold on Sunday at 1:30 AM. I found myself unable to sleep. So I got up and went to the living room to read and picked up a magazine.

I have a habit of reading magazines from the back to the front and did so that night. That particular magazine had several pages of Classified Ads in the back, so I started to read them hoping that they would make me drowsy and put me to sleep. They almost did until I came across an ad that grabbed my attention. I couldn't believe my eyes. I read it again and again.

I wanted to stay up all night, but I did get some sleep and then held off until 6 AM Denver time to call the New York number at 8 AM.

Here was the answer to my question: "How could I market my book to the rest of the people in the United States and help them get the jobs they really wanted?"

The Ad?

Authors Wanted for Radio Talk Shows,
Call 212-xxx-xxxx.

I read it again and again. I even circled it with a red felt marker just to make sure I wouldn't lose it.

I looked at the clock, only 2:05 AM . . . nearly 4 hours before I could call the business number.

It was a long night.

I tried to go back to sleep, but in my excited state sleep wasn't possible. So I read for several more hours. Periodically I'd turn back to the classified ad (circled in red) to make sure it was still there.

At 6:01 AM (8:01 New York time) I called the number. I didn't get a secretary or a receptionist. Instead I got the president of the company. I asked him several questions about his ad. He answered them all telling me he was a publicist. It was his business to book authors on radio talk shows.

He explained that he booked authors for radio talk show interviews and charged them $60 per show.

I was ready to say, "Give me three shows." He countered with, "That's with a 20-show minimum."

Gulp! That's a BIG $1,200 commitment. He went on to say that he guaranteed his work and gave me the names and phone numbers of several authors as references.

After checking his references, I mailed my new publicist $1,200 and 20 copies of my book. Within three weeks he had me booked for 20 shows.

He called back to ask, "Do you want to do it again?" I replied, "Yes." He said, "$75 per show."

Another gulp. That's $1,500! He asked me if it was worth it. It was. I was selling an average of 35-40 books per show. That was more than $500 in retail sales on each show.

So I sent him $1,500 and 20 more books.

After the second 20 interviews, my publicist asked, "Do you want to do it again?" This time I asked, "How much?" His answer was $100 per show.

That's when I said, "Thanks, but No Thanks."

That, my friend, is when and why I created the **Radio Talk Show System.** The book you are now holding in your hand is but one part of this system.

Over a period of four months I invested nearly $4,000 in telephone calls to find the stations that were willing to interview guests by telephone.

In addition I invested days and weeks perfecting my radio talk show presentation. I also found an answering service that was able to take calls from all over the U.S.

Here's how you are really saving money.

I've designed this book to save you over $5,000 (which is now the going price for a publicist) and enable you to do this for yourself.

Would I do it over again? You bet. When I want to do something and I don't have the answer or expertise, I find it pays to find specialists in the field and pay them for their expertise and experience. Then I learn from it.

Now, let's talk about how to get started. These are principles that work for us each day, and they can work for you, too.

Chapter 3

Who Needs Radio Talk Show Guests and Why?

Did you know . . .

★ Every day in America 280 million people turn on the radio?

★ 99% of Americans have a radio in their home, their car or their office?

Think about this. Do you ever go anyplace in your car without turning on the radio? Or is your car radio ALWAYS turned on? Ask your friends, neighbors and family. You'll be amazed at how radio oriented our society is today.

On many of these radio stations, there is a phenomenon sweeping America today called **Radio Talk Shows.** You can capitalize on the talk radio trend as easily as I have.

Here's the total count of radio stations in America as of April 2011.

4,778 Commercial AM stations

9,950 Commercial FM stations

For a total of 14,728 radio stations.

Next questions:

★ Which of these 14,728 radio stations have a talk show format?

★ Which have the capability to conduct interviews with guests by **telephone**?

★ And finally, why do these stations need **you**?

In the times in which we're living I've discovered that the public wants **Instant Information and Controversy.** Radio stations have picked up on this phenomenon. Many stations are converting some of their programming to talk shows and some stations to All Talk Formats.

Radio stations are always in a ratings contest with each other. Talk radio seems to be the key for radio stations to capture and hold their audience for more than just one song. Radio stations, therefore, are adding good talk show hosts to their payrolls. Also producers are needed to maintain full scheduling.

What else do they need?

Now, here's where you and I come in. For talk shows to exist and expand their listening base, **good talk show guests are vitally important and necessary.**

For instance, one show host in Pittsburgh, PA uses (needs) 135 guests per month. And there are at least five other hosts on the same station.

How many guests are needed per station? How many guests are needed all over the U.S.? The number is in the tens of thousands.

In the meantime, don't worry about guests running out of shows on which to talk. It will be a long time before that happens.

To illustrate just how important radio talk show guests are, here's an experience I had on a trip to Florida where I was invited to speak to the Florida Publishers Association, I learned what is meant by the expression "open lines."

As is my custom, whenever I am driving I turn the radio dial to the AM stations and start scanning the dial for a talk show. There it was at 1600 AM - an all talk station.

It was five minutes before the top of the hour and I had a 20-minute drive ahead to get to Punta Gorda. I sat back ready to enjoy listening to a new host on a new station.

The host, named Joe, was closing this segment of his program with the statement, "Folks, when we return from the news and weather, you can call in and talk about any subject you'd like . . . sports, elections. You get to choose the subject. We're going to have **open lines**."

I patiently listened to the news and the weather. At 5:05 PM host Joe came back asking his listeners, "Well folks, what would you like to talk about? We now have open lines."

Results? No one called in. Joe talked to himself for the next 15 minutes and not ONE caller.

I wanted to pull over to the side of the road to call Joe at the station and say: "Let's talk about *How to Get the Job You Really Want and Get Employers to Call You.*" I didn't. But I believe you're getting the message. Talk show hosts need Guests (you and me).

The lesson here? People (listeners) need someone to "prime the pump." They need good guests like you and me to address a specific subject. Then everyone's job becomes easier. The host or hostess has someone with whom to talk. The listeners can then relate to a specific topic. The guest also benefits with an almost unlimited audience.

I've invested hundreds of hours and thousands of dollars to identify the list of stations that have talk shows and need guests like you and me.

After being interviewed on over 723 talk shows, here's what I've found so far:

1. My average Radio Talk Show is 30 minutes in length.
2. An average of 3 persons call in with questions.
3. An average of 35% of all the listeners who are tuned in to the program go to my website and order my Jobs Book.

KACHING!

What will your numbers be? There's only one way to find out. As the Nike commercial says: "Just Do It!" Get started NOW. Here's how you can turn your idea into money. And you can do this without leaving your home or office.

Are you ready? Let's help talk shows eliminate those troublesome open lines.

Chapter 4

Deciding on What to Talk About

Every year for over 20 years I have been updating my Talk Show database.

Each time I talk with either a host or producer I ask the same question: "Exactly what are you looking for?"

The answers always came out the same: "Either FREE Information or something controversial."

Then this year I noticed that most hosts and producers have added a third category.

"We'd really like someone who is PASSIONATE ABOUT THEIR SUBJECT."

That's the key: Passion. Passion for your subject. The passion to want to help listeners of talk radio.

What do you have to offer listeners?

Experience has shown that the one item radio talk show listeners want most of all is — **information**.

You read it right — INFORMATION on a whole variety of subjects.

Recently I asked a talk show producer, "What are the hottest topics for this year?" His reply: "Either Free Information, Something Controversial, or especially a subject on which someone is passionate."

Some of the hottest topics are:
★ Money - how to make it.
★ Money - how to save it. (People, especially business people, are all bottom-line oriented.)
★ Health - how to become more healthy, how to stay healthy.
★ Relationships - how to attract members of the opposite sex or how to win friends.
★ Happiness - ideas to improve on their present level of happiness.

Other topics I've heard recently include:
★ How to Lose Weight
★ Using Hypnosis to Get Rid of Bad Habits
★ How to Use Your Natural Voice

Research the news – on the internet, in the newspaper, and on TV to see 'what's hot.'

There is an unlimited supply of ideas and topics addressed on radio talk shows. To get an idea about what topics are covered, try this.

Find a popular radio station in your area that has an all talk format. You can do this by going to www.Radio-Locator.com. Then a phone call to several radio stations will help you find the #1 or #2 best talk show radio station in your area. Then for one week keep your car and wake-up alarm radios tuned to that station. Start listening to the various shows.

Each host will be offering a different general subject; such as psychology, sports, home and gardening, automotive, health, psychic phenomena . . . the list goes on and on.

Keep a note pad beside your radio or in your car. Make notes to yourself of the names and topics of the various guests you hear on these shows. You'll be amazed at the diversity.

As varied as they are, they all have one thing in common. Radio talk show guests are people who are capable of speaking on any of these topics and offering their opinions. They are also able to field questions and interact with the listeners and the host.

The odds are that by now you are listening to the still small voice inside you saying: "Hey, I've got several topics that I am qualified to speak on. Why not me? I deserve to be on those radio talk shows!"

Of course you not only deserve to be on Radio Talk Shows. You can be. Radio talk shows need a lot of guests. Why not YOU?

Think of your area of expertise. What subjects are you most interested in? What do you know more about than 95% of the population?

> **ONLY, ONLY, ONLY, speak on something you've earned the right to speak about through your own experience or your education.**

I learned this valuable lesson while taking the Dale Carnegie Course more than 30 years ago. The instructors repeated Dale Carnegie's advice over and over again.

Keep in mind that you don't have to be **the** expert on the subject, just informed enough so that you can talk knowledgeably about the subject for some time. No one out there in the listening audience expects you to know **everything** there is to know on your subject. But, you should have some firm opinions and be extremely interested in your subject and able to convey this information fluently in a professional manner. If your information is in the "How to" category so much the better.

Once you have decided on what you will be talking about, the next step is to get your ideas into a format such as a book, CD, DVD or Tip Sheet. I will explain how I did so in the next chapter; for you, too, can turn your ideas into a money making venture.

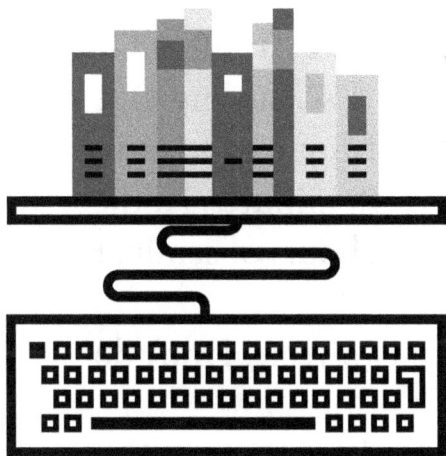

Chapter 5

Getting Your Ideas Into Book Format

Talk show listeners are looking for **additional information** from the guests being interviewed.

They want specific answers to specific questions they have on the subject.

This additional information can take shape in several formats. For example,

★ Do you have a manuscript on your desk?

★ Have you written a book?

★ Are you published?

★ Have you written a report or tip sheet?

★ Is there a beginning of a pamphlet in your mind on a topic of interest to you?

★ Have you recorded and duplicated CDs or DVDs for distribution?

A prolific writer I am not. I do not sit down at a typewriter or computer and have the words just flow through my fingers. This may work for some people, but not for me. I don't work that way.

To get the first copy of the jobs book on paper I took a totally different route. If you'll remember I told you that in 1979 I put this jobs information into a seminar format. In 1980 while conducting an all-day version of this seminar, I set up my tape recorder on the table in the first row and had my two friends, Jim and Dana Melton, change the tapes every 30 minutes. At the end of the day I had six tapes with a total of six hours of seminar information on them.

I carried these tapes around for more than two years. Don't do that!

Finally, I found a friend who loves to type. Betty is an editor but temporarily without a typewriter. I had a typewriter but I had no experience in transcribing tapes.

So, we did a trade. Betty got to use my typewriter and in return she transcribed these tapes into a rough draft copy of the first manuscript. Then came the editing and revisions to make my spoken words more readable.

I discovered that I don't have to be a writing whiz to get this information down on paper.

The key here is to find out:

What Works for You
  ★ Your forte may be speaking. So you may prefer to use a digital recorder as you speak.
  ★ Some folks find that writing longhand is their best style.
  ★ Others write better using a computer.

Find what works best for you. Whatever it takes, I encourage you, don't delay. Get your material into some kind of format — book, CD, etc. that you can put into the hands of your listeners. **Do it, and do it now!!**

Keep in mind that if you write a book, to become "published" does not necessarily mean that a New York publisher accepts your book and turns it into a best seller.

Becoming published can be done in one of several ways and can mean being:

★ Published by a traditional publishing house

★ Print on Demand published

★ Independently-published

The most popular of these today is the independently-published route. It is also the quickest, most cost effective and in most cases the **most profitable**.

When I decided to put my jobs seminar information into written form, that is transcribing the tapes which became my first manuscript, I sent the manuscript off to six New York publishers.

The result? Six Rejection Letters.

So rather than wait and hope for a contract from a major publisher, which is nearly every writer's goal and dream, I self-published my book, *How to Get the Job You Really Want and Get Employers to Call You.*

My goal was to get this "jobs information" into the hands of as many people as possible as soon as possible. I wanted to help thousands of persons get the **job they really wanted right now!**

Self Publishing vs New York Publishing?

You decide.

After being interviewed on 723 radio talk shows, I sold more than 23,750 copies of *How to Get the Job You Really Want and Get Employers to Call You*. That's more than $376,000 worth of books.

I then received an offer from a New York publisher. Their offer? If I'd let them publish my book, they would give me a $25,000 advance.

After much discussion, including the fact that my book was in only one bookstore, I felt that with their distribution system, my book would now be in bookstores and libraries all across America.

This would give my book a good chance of reaching tens of thousands of people I would never have reached by radio talk shows only.

So I said, "YES!"

They did a good job. With very little editing they republished my book in an 8-1/2" x 5-1/2" format, designed to fit purses and brief cases.

After nearly three years, they sold a total of 7,100 books.

Yes, I appreciated the $25,000 advance, but I hadn't received any royalties.

I had also given up the daily income stream I had created by marketing my book via radio talk shows. ($7-8,000 a month).

Is this a Good News/Bad News story? Only you can decide.

My New York publisher decided to NOT go back to press. They returned the rights to my book back to me.

With some updating and minor editing, I was ready to "Roll It Out Again," as a self-published author.

Would I publish again with a major publisher? Probably not.

New York publishing certainly may fit the needs of authors with name recognition and mass distribution.

But for beginning authors/publishers, using this radio talk show system gives them the ability to build a daily income stream.

The profit margin allows them to do many things themselves that New York publishing does not allow.

The three magic words in my vocabulary?

Test ★ Test ★ Test

All good things come to those who Wait . . . and Hustle while they are waiting.

There will never be a better time for you to add AUTHOR to whatever other credentials you presently possess. In my case AUTHOR/SPEAKER is 10 times more powerful and credible than just SPEAKER alone.

Believe me when I say this. The America public puts authors up on pedestals. People ohh and ahh when they meet an "author." And **you can be an author** in a very short period of time if you follow the steps above.

Here is one of the best resources I know of for Independent Publishing: *The Self Publishing Manual: How To Write, Print & Sell Your Own Book* by Dan Poynter
Para Publishing, Santa Barbara, California
www.ParaPub.com

You'll also find more books at your favorite book store or library.

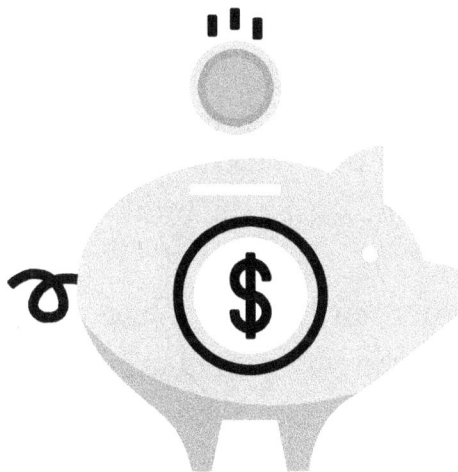

Chapter 6

Turning Your Book Into a Money Machine

Getting a book published is just the first step. Now you've got to find the natural market for your book.

Here's a longer range picture of how my book evolved.

My self-published book has taken several formats. At first it was photocopied and in a spiral bound format. Several hundred copies were sold that way.

Next, I re-typeset the book in an 8-1/2" x 5-1/2" format. A limited run of these quickly showed me that this was not as effective as the 8-1/2" x 11" format, so I returned to the full-page size.

When deciding which format is best for you, I encourage you to

Test, Test, Test!

My book was originally 60 pages in length in an 8 1/2" x 11" format, with a two-color cover, and saddle stitched (stapled). Now, it's 92 pages, with a four-color cover and perfect bound (with a spine).

Here are a few tips that have helped me get this book into local bookstores.

Getting local publicity via radio talk shows in my city was most important. I was invited back twice by my original talk show host after the initial interview I described in Chapter One. These repeat performances helped me get my book into the bookstore that is the largest in the U.S.

Before appearing on the local talk show here in Denver, I had visited the Tattered Cover Bookstore. I asked the buyer in charge of career books if she would be interested in carrying my book.

She looked the book over (back to front) and thumbed through the pages in an attempt to get a "feel" for the book. She was kind as she handed it back to me and said, "It's a nice book, Mr. Sabah, but I'm sorry, we can't carry your book."

When I asked her why, she explained: "First, all books **must** have an ISBN number (International Standard Book Number.) This is how bookstores keep track of their inventory. And second, your book is stapled (saddle stitched) and would not display well. The customers have to be able to see the title on the spine. We'd have to display your book face-out and my limited shelf space won't permit that."

About four weeks later (after appearing on the local talk show mentioned above), I received a phone call from this same person at the book store. She explained that she had received several requests for my book. Would I bring down five copies and leave them with her on consignment. (This means if they sell, I get paid. If they don't sell, the books are returned.)

I delivered five books to her on Monday. On Friday I received a phone call from a student named Carl, who had enrolled for my **Jobs Seminar.**

Carl wanted to know where he could purchase the book so that he could get a head start on the seminar. I proudly gave Carl the phone number of the Tattered Cover bookstore that carried my book.

Within two hours he called me back saying: "I'm at the Tattered Cover and they are all **out** of your books."

I asked him to let me talk to Dottie, the person in charge of career books. Dottie asked me to deliver six more copies **again on consignment**. I happily obliged. She had the check waiting for me for the first five copies.

The next six sold in less than two weeks. The next order was for ten copies, then 15, then 25 at a time.

In 12 months, the Tattered Cover sold over 400 copies of my book.

The next step was to get the ISBN number that Dottie said all books needed.

If you are independently publishing your own book, here's how easy it is to get an ISBN (International Standard Book Number). Simply go to www.ISBN.org. Be very careful of others selling these numbers. This is the only place to get your own original numbers. If you purchase them from another company online or elsewhere, whoever originally purchased the number from ISBN.org is now the Publisher of record.

This ISBN number has helped not only bookstores keep track of my book, but also in my marketing.

My book was originally published in a staple-bound format . . . it is now published in a perfect-bind format and in its fifth printing.

This story reminds me of one of the mini post cards that I print and distribute by the tens of thousands:

> **You don't have to be good to start —
> But you have to start — to be good!**

Proper Pricing of Your Book or Product

What price should I charge for my book when it is sold via radio talk shows?

Should the price include shipping and handling or should I quote this item separately?

What about guarantees? Won't guarantees result in a lot of refunds?

The information in this section could easily result in the difference between profit OR loss for you.

Item #1 – you will want to have done your homework as outlined above. That is, listen to as many radio talk shows as possible. Make notes of the products they are offering and the pricing structure.

What dollar 'range' do most of the items offered fall in? Are shipping and handling quoted separately or INCLUDED in the price mentioned?

Experience has shown that people respond better when they have only ONE number to remember. You should always add "and that includes shipping and handling."

In establishing the price to charge for your book or product, keep the following in mind. When selling by radio talk shows you will want to figure in the cost of maintaining your web site, the credit card charges, plus, the costs of shipping and handling.

Shipping could be the cost to ship via USPS (United States Postal Service), UPS (United Parcel Service) or possibly even FedEx (Federal Express).

I use USPS Priority Mail. As of this printing, I can send my book anywhere in the US in two days for $6.45.

Handling can include the packaging: envelope, address labels, to and from, stickers for indicating type of mail (First Class, etc.) and, of course, the labor to get the package in the mail and on its way to your buyers.

As a result a book that might sell for $7.95 in a retail store could be priced at $12.95 on radio talk shows.

A $12 book at retail could be priced at $17.95. I have included the following worksheet to assist you in deciding what price to charge for your book or CD:

Worksheet to Figure the Proper Selling Price of Your Product

Cost of Goods to be Sold
  (price you pay for producing your product) $_____
Multiplied by 4 or 5 = $_____
In other words this is your retail price which
should always be 4 or 5 times what it cost you
to produce your product
                Plus:
                Shipping $_____
                Handling $_____
                Envelope/packaging $_____
                Labels, from and to $_____
                Labor $_____
                Credit Card Charges $_____

                TOTAL $_____

Chapter 7

Becoming a Credit Card Merchant

There are various ways to accept credit cards:

1. Through your bank – talk to the business department

2. Online, via PayPal, GooglePay or various Merchant Services

3. Through your cell phone/tablet with Apps such as *Square*

Do your research and find the easiest ways for you to sell your products and/or services with credit card capabilities.

Chapter 8

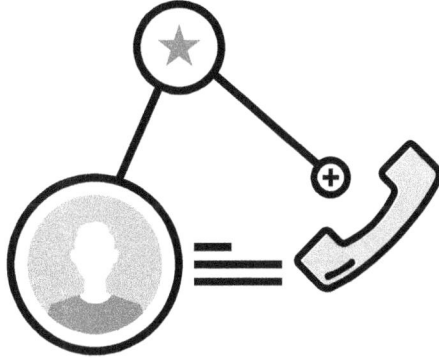

Using the Telephone to Book Radio Talk Shows

The very best method of achieving results in booking radio talk shows is to **use the telephone and call the radio stations.** I have found that it helps to write down what you intend to say before you call; in other words, **a script.**

What follows is a script to give you some idea of what may happen when you call a radio station.

Of course, you will want to develop your own script after making several calls and discovering what works best for you.

Here goes!

First call:

Receptionist: "Radio Station KXYZ."

You: "May I speak with _____ (usually the producer), please?

"Hello, _____, my name is _____.

I understand that you are in charge of scheduling guests for the _____ show. Is that correct?

(In selling you want your prospect to say "Yes" early and often.)

"The reason for my call, _____ (their first name) is:

"I am the author of a book on the subject of

_____,

or entitled: _____.

I believe this information **will get your phone ringing and help your listeners to . . ."**

(Give them 3 quick benefits here.)

1. _____

2. _____

3. _____

"Is this the type of subject that you and your host are looking for?" or "Could this subject help the listeners of your show?"

Sounds easy, doesn't it?

Let me back up two steps and give you several tips that will make your life easier and more productive.

Tip #1 – The odds of you getting through to the host or the producer on your first call, are pretty slim. I've found that the best times to call is from one hour before the show time to one hour after the show time. They generally do not stay in the studio the whole day.

When you call the station you may get a response such as, "He/she is not in." Or you may be told, "He/she is on the air. Would you like to leave a message on his/her voice mail?" Just remember this phrase. **The person who makes the call stays in control.**

Rather than leaving messages on voice mail or with the station's receptionist, you will want to say, **"No thank you, what is the best time for me to call them back?"** Jot this time down in your appointment book, and call back when they are most likely to be in.

Your first call will have taken about 30-45 seconds. So your first round of calls will be to schedule telephone appointments for the next day.

This is truly a voicemail world. Remember most people are NOT sitting by their phones waiting for us to call.

Just keep in mind that radio talk shows and their hosts **need you!** There is a tremendous need for guests every day of the year.

One day I received a call from Dan B., a producer in Pittsburgh, PA. Dan was calling to ask me to be a guest on his host's show.

My reply? "Dan, this will be my third appearance on your show.

How many guests do you need?"

He answered: "Let's see. My host Scott is on the air three hours a day and needs a new guest each hour." That's 15 guests a week, or about 65 guests a month.

His host is only one of five hosts on this particular station. Just think, 325 guests a year for one host. That's 1,575 guests for five hosts in one year. And that's for only one station.

Do they need you and me? You bet!

Read on to find out how to multiply yourself by . . .

Hiring and training an effective phone person

Tip #2 – after you've accomplished your own booking, you'll probably be too busy conducting the talk show interviews to continue booking yourself.

Here's where you multiply your efforts by finding, hiring, training and supervising an effective phone person to do the booking for you.

This person can be worth his or her weight in gold.

To find the **right** person you should:

Step #1 - Find someone who LOVES the phone, and

Step #2 - This person should be thoroughly familiar with you and your material. They should have read your book and be excited about your message.

Here's an idea. Have your new telephone appointment person attend a seminar you are conducting, or at a minimum read your book, or listen to the audio CD materials you are offering. This person should be so familiar with you and your material that he/ she is capable of answering almost any questions about you that they are asked.

Step #3 - Prepare a script for this person to use.

You mean exact words? **Yes, exact words.**

Engineered words designed to get a specified result at the right time. This is the key to getting the results you want: **Radio Talk Show Bookings.**

Step #4 - Train this person yourself. Train by example by having this person sit and listen to you while you make several calls. You have learned how to make these calls pay off with bookings. Now, you have the opportunity to demonstrate the **right way.** People learn by example.

Step #5 - Next, ask your new talk show booking person to make several calls while you observe. After each call take the time to review and comment on what your phone booking person did right.

Also analyze areas in which improvements can be made.

Step #6 - Have your phone person make an hour of phone calls unobserved. Then monitor the results of those calls. If they did not result in at least one booking, go back to step #5.

The Radio Talk Show Confirmation Sheet (Chapter 9) is one part of the record keeping system. To help you supervise your phone person you will also want to have them keep a daily tally of:

★ No. of calls made = Even if they get a busy signal or no answer.

★ Contacts made = A hello by a receptionist.

★ Key person = Talking to the host or producer.

★ More information sent = Interested enough to ask for more information, but no booking yet.

★ Bookings = Confirmed talk show bookings with a date and time for you to be a guest.

These tallies should be kept by the hour. This way you can help identify calling patterns and results by the time of day and day of the week. This will certainly improve your efficiency and monitoring of the calls.

The process of hiring a telephone booking person described above is becoming more cost effective in business circles. Some business people call this person their "Personal Assistant." A properly hired and trained Personal Assistant can certainly help you improve the productivity and profitability of your business.

This system works . . . if you do. Keep in mind, that whether you or your assistant makes that call, calling is still the most effective way to book radio talk shows.

Using the telephone is ALWAYS the best way to book talk shows. The second best way is to send an email.

If you are going to email Producers, use a CRM, a customer relationship management program, like MailChimp.com that allows you to personalize each record. This will help you to get a better open rate. DO NOT use a running paragraph. Use bullets with white space and benefit, benefit, benefit (similar to the PR postcard in Chapter 10).

Always remember that talk radio is an interactive auditory medium.

Chapter 9

Radio Talk Show Confirmation Sheets

You will want to keep track of your radio talk show bookings.

After working with a variety of forms, from 3x5 cards to legal size sheets, I have created the ideal way to keep track of bookings. I then created my own forms, the "Radio Talk Show Confirmation Sheet."

A supply of these forms is at the corner my desk. The minute I get a phone call from a talk show producer or host, I have this form at my fingertips, ready to capture the information to book my next Radio Talk Show. This form is organized so that I have a flow of the 'right' questions to ask this person.

The Radio Talk Show Confirmation Sheet is arranged to enable you to capture the name of the contact person.

This person is usually the producer or the host of the show. Some hosts produce their own shows (even on the larger stations).

Make certain that you get this person's name right as well as the correct spelling. If you did not hear the person's name the first time, ask him/her to repeat it or better yet spell it for you.

Dale Carnegie teaches "a man or woman's name to them is the sweetest and most important sound in any language." After you get the name and title/position, make sure that you use their name throughout the call.

Instead of asking, "What station are you with?" try this. "Thanks for calling me, Sally. With what station are you associated?"

Get not only the call letters, but also the exact name of the show on which you are being booked. Find out the title or position this person holds with that station.

Other take charge questions are:

★ "What dates are you looking to fill?"
★ "How long is your host on the air?"
★ "Is that Eastern time/Central time/Mountain time/ Pacific time?"
★ "Are you an hour ahead of me? (or two hours behind me?)"
★ "How long a time slot are you looking to fill?"
★ "Will you have callers during this program?"
★ "To whose attention should I send a copy of my book?" (only if they ask.)
★ "Do I understand correctly? You will be calling me?"
★ "Let me give you the number to call me."

Other Questions I Find Valuable

★ "What are your call letters?"
★ "Are you on AM, FM or both?"
★ "What frequency are you at on the dial . . . in case I want to notify friends in your city to listen?"
★ "On how many watts do you operate?" (50,000 watters - AM - are the most powerful.)

Before you hang up the phone, you will want to reconfirm all the above information. Repeat back to your caller the date (and **day** of week), time (and **length** of program) and whether the time is YOUR time zone or theirs, who will call whom, the correct phone number. Also, repeat back the address and name of the person to receive a copy of your book/product.

The three keys words here are **confirm, confirm, confirm!!!**

Never leave anything to chance.

Cover all of your bases.

Be professional.

On the next page is a copy of my **Radio Talk Show Confirmation Sheet:**

Radio Talk Show Confirmation Sheet

Today's Date: _____/_____/_____

Station Call Letters _____

AM __ FM __ Watts _____

Name of Contact: _____

Name of Show: _____

Name of Host: _____

Date of Interview: _____

Day of Interview: _____

Time of Interview: (Your Time) _____

How Long: _____ Minutes

They Call me: YES NO   I call them: YES NO

Address of Station: _____

City/State/ZIP: _____

Station Phone Number: _____

Producer Email: _____

Date book sent out: _____/_____/_____

Additional Comments: _____

_____

_____

Date input into your database: _____/_____/_____

After each show I track the exact number of books sold and record that number on this form. I also keep track of the number of shows I've been on, the number of minutes per show, and the names of the callers with whom we talk.

Next, I enter the details of this form into my database. The reason for this is threefold:

1. **To keep good business records.**
2. **To follow up after the show with a Thank-You Card (see example in Chapter 16).**
3. **To reschedule another show 3 to 6 months later.**

Keeping good records will help you make more money.

Here's how to further multiply your effectiveness.

Have a master calendar on your office wall. Three or four months ahead is a good time frame with which to work.

Next, highlight with a bright marker the dates and times that are already booked, either for speaking engagements, business or work.

Now you are free to let your Personal Assistant know that you are available for the balance of the unmarked times for RADIO TALK SHOWS.

How busy do you want to be? That is a question that only **you** can answer.

I've tried one or two shows a week. Results? When too much time elapsed between shows I found I was out of practice.

I tried one show a day. That was a piece of cake.

I've done as many as five shows in one day. That was too heavy a schedule for me.

My best format? Two shows a day. One in the AM. One in the PM. This way I stay on my toes.

Cavett Robert, founder of the National Speakers Association, once told me that it is easier to speak once a day than to speak once a month.

Have enough shows scheduled so that you are always in top form. You enjoy the flow of questions from the listeners. You anticipate the enthusiasm that is generated by another show in several hours.

This works and is **fun!**

Ready for the **fun** part?

Chapter 10

Creating a PR Postcard That Gets Fabulous Results

As promised in Chapter 2, here is:

"Why Goldenrod May Be a Stroke of Genius"

Does Goldenrod paper really work? Does color really sell?

On Valentine's Day I was scheduled to appear on a Southern California talk show. The previous guest was running overtime, so the producer asked if I would be willing to wait for five minutes. They were minutes from finishing their previous interview.

It was during this interview that I learned a Most Valuable Lesson. The guest was from the Color Institute of America. The host asked whether the institute had ever done a survey on various colors and their impact on "results."

She told of a survey where a company had mailed out 10,000 sales letters all on White. She went on to say: "Let's use 100 for the results on White paper."

The same letter or offer was mailed to 10,000 on Blue paper.

The results? 112. Then another 10,000 were mailed out on Pink paper. Results? 124. And finally, when they mailed out 10,000 letters on Goldenrod paper, the results: 142 responses!

WOW! A 42% greater return just by changing the color of paper. Same offer — just brighter paper.

That's when I started asking myself the question: Why does Goldenrod outsell any other color?

Think along with me. What color do they paint all the school buses in America? Bright yellow (or nearly goldenrod.)

What color does the highway department paint the Yield Signs on the highways? Black on Yellow.

McDonald's Restaurants have the money to paint their signs any color they want. Why did they choose "Golden Arches"?

If you're like me, you already have the answer.

Anytime you want to capture someone's attention you use color; especially the sharpest contract - Black on Goldenrod.

If it works for school buses, highway signs, and McDonalds, wouldn't it also work for you and me?

In the course of a year's time, I find that my use of colored paper and cardstock is many, many times that of white paper.

Years ago a friend advised that it only costs a few cents more to go First Class! In this case First Class gets greater results, for just a fraction more.

Now you know the "Secret" of the GOLD FORM. Let's put that knowledge to work.

★ ★ ★ ★ ★

Postcards Work!

Wow! I wondered what would happen if I used my son Joe's Gold Form to create a Giant Postcard?

You won't have to wonder. Read on to find a useful PR piece.

Just think – all you have to do is put a First Class stamp, plus a mailing label on this card and drop it in the mail. No envelope, no cover letter is required. And when your Host or Producer receives this Giant Postcard it's already open and ready to read. Postcards seem to get top priority over envelopes when mail is received.

This 5 ½" x 8 ½" Giant Gold Postcard works. I've kept track of results. I got a 6% return, which means that out of every 100 Giant Gold Postcards I mailed to radio stations, 6 of these stations called to book me.

KACHING!

Several Hosts have told me, "You won't have to send me your one-sheet or book. I have enough information on this card to interview you. Let's set up an interview for day after tomorrow."

Now, that's action, wouldn't you agree?

I've been blessed with a very creative and fertile mind. I never let a day go by without giving thanks to God for this blessing. So, from time to time, you can expect to be hearing from me about other new ideas you can use to increase your promotional activities.

Remember: This oversized postcard requires a first Class stamp (in the US). The traditional postcard rate is good only for a maximum size of 4x6 inches.

A sample of the Giant PR Postcard I use is on the next page. Use your creativity to make this idea work for you.

Postage

Joe Sabah
PO Box 101330
Denver, CO 80250
303-722-7200

Return Service Requested

Your phone will ring off the hook when you interview the author of this book:

How to Get the Job You REALLY Want . . .
And Get Employers to Call You"

Joe Sabah welcomes calls from your listeners and will help them:
1. Decide what they really want to do
2. Create their own Golf Form that gets employers to call them
3. Turn every job interview into a job offer using the 3 Magic Steps

Producer
Station
Address
City, State, Zip

Turn Me
Over **F-A-S-T**
For Information
to Book This Guest

51

AVAILABLE IMMEDIATELY . . . .

Joe Sabah

Dynamic, Articulate Talk Show Guest

Joe is an Author, Professional Speaker and Consultant

He will help your listeners get their ideal jobs

1. It all started when Joe helped his son, Joe, get 3 job offers in 72 hours . . . even though his son lived 1,200 miles away
2. Joe loves telling the story of how Linda S received 10 job offers from the **"Gold Form"** and went from earning $28,.000 a year as a School Teacher to earning $75,000 a year as a Wholesaler
3. Joe says, "Resumes don't work! If resumes worked . . . everyone in America would have a job. **Use the Gold Form instead. It works . . . by Getting Employers to Call YOU!"**
4. Joe's favorite part of the interview is when he is able to answer questions from listeners in your city
5. Let Joe share with your listening audience the 3 steps that he promises will turn every job interview into a job offer.

Why invite Joe Sabah to be your guest?

Timely Topic – How TO GET THE JOB YOU REALLY WANT . . .
AND GET EMPLOYERS TO CALL YOU

Your listeners will gain . . .
1. Information for marketing themselves in today's job market
2. New, innovative, creative ideas to - Get Employers to Call Them
3. A 3-step approach to turn every job interview into a JOB OFFER

Call 303-722-7200 and book Joe Sabah Today

When you call to book Joe, be sure to request your copy of the E-Book:
How to Get the Job You Really Want and Get Employers to Call You

Joe Sabah
PO Box 101330
Denver, CO 80250
303-722-7200

Chapter 11

Confirming Your Radio Interview

You've talked to the Producer. You've set up a time for them to call and interview you. Now what?

When confirming your interview with a Producer, ask for their email address. Send a confirmation IMMEDIATELY with "Confirming our interview" in the Subject line. This will ensure that your email does not get mixed up with any of the SPAM email they receive.

Format it like this:

From: Your email address

To: Producers email address

Subject: Confirming my interview on the <show> program on <date and time>

Body of email:

Hi, <Producer>,

It was nice talking with you today. This is to confirm my interview with <Host> on <Date and Time with time zone included>.

I understand that you will be calling me 5 minutes before the show at xxx-xxx-xxxx.

To make the interview go more smoothly, here are 10 questions to ask about How to Get the Job You Really Want and Get Employers to Call You.

In the meantime, should you have any questions, you can call me at xxx-xxx-xxxx or email me at Joe@JoeSabah.com.

(The following is the "Questions to Ask Sheet" I send to the host in my confirmation email):

Questions to ask Joe Sabah about
How to Get The Job You Really Want and
Get Employers to Call You

1. How did you conceive the idea for the book?

2. What if a person doesn't know what they want to do?

3. Can this book help people over 40?

4. You mention **Interviewing for Information** in your book, tell us about that.

5. If you don't use resumes what do you use?

6. Tell me more about the "Gold Form."

7. Why don't you list past jobs on the Gold Form?

8. In your book, you give a three-step formula that you guarantee will turn every job interview into a job offer. Will you tell our listeners what those three steps are?

9. How do you **get the employers to call you?**

10. Tell us, how can a person get their name to the top of the list of applicants?

Hosts will appreciate your thoughtfulness in providing these questions. Most often these are the same questions the host would be asking you anyway. But your anticipation in providing them with questions will help make you appear as the PROFESSIONAL you are.

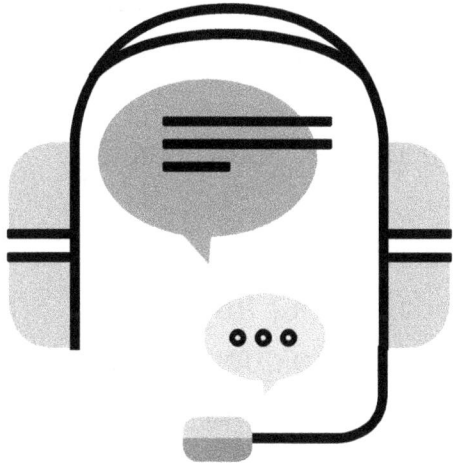

Chapter 12

Structuring a Successful Radio Talk Show Interview

Here's how to structure a **successful** radio talk show interview.

Believe me when I tell you there is a **BIG** difference between **just** a radio talk show interview and a **successful** radio talk show interview. Small tips make a **BIG** difference. Here are some tips that I've learned that made the **BIG** difference.

Prepare the area you will be using for your talk show interviews. This means be relaxed, but not too comfortable.

Check the latest in headsets. For only $50-150 you can purchase a cordless headset, allowing you TOTAL freedom to walk and talk. Check your local Electronics Store.

I find it most stimulating to stand and walk while I am talking on the telephone . . . especially when I'm being interviewed on a talk show. This is my style in speaking in seminars. You, of course, will develop your own style.

During your next phone call, take the call while you are seated.

Notice how you sometimes cradle the phone on your shoulder. This may cause your voice to be muffled. Your shoulders may be slouched over, causing your chest cavity to be sunken. Results? A less than effective phone call.

Next call: Stand up before answering your phone. Stand erect. Be comfortable. Pace if that is your style.

Notice the difference? More confidence. More power. More sales. Always have a copy of your book/material at your fingertips.

Paperclip or highlight the passages that you want to quote from.

Use Post-It notes to "flag" important passages from your book.

Keep a glass of water handy. This helps in case you feel a cough coming on. Some speakers suggest warm or even room temperature water. Coffee? Tea? Not my style, but try it. See what works best for you.

Posted on your wall or desk somewhere should be the three (ONLY 3) key points that you want to cover in this interview.

My 3 points are:

1. How to decide what you want to do occupationally.
2. How to get employers to call you.
3. Three tips guaranteed to turn every job interview into a job offer.

(See Chapter 14 for details on how to cover three points in five minutes vs 55 minutes.)

Plus, post the website you want to give your listeners to call at the end of the program.

The three key points mentioned above can also be posed as questions. These questions are a valuable part of the confirmation you send the Talk Show Host ahead of time.

Chapter 13

Getting the Most Out of YOUR Talk Show Interview

Here are some valuable tips to make your talk show presentation ideal:

1. Get rid of distractions: kids, pets, family, radio, TV.

2. Have a nice quiet place from which to talk.

3. Get in a comfortable position. I prefer standing and pacing as though I'm conducting a seminar.

4. Use stories, especially success stories from people who have used the ideas from your book or CDs.

5. Use quotes from your book, and always refer to page numbers.

Here's another idea to improve the quality of your talk shows:

When a person calls in **always, always** ask for his or her first name. Do NOT refer to the person as "Caller." This is strictly amateurish, and smacks of not caring enough about your listeners who call in to pay close enough attention to them to get their first names. **Use their first name in responding to their question.**

In all professional speaker training programs, speakers (and talk show guests) are taught to repeat the caller's question and compliment them for asking such an intelligent/provocative question. Repeating their question does 3 things:

1. It clarifies the question in your mind and in the mind of the caller.

2. It allows other listeners to empathize with the first caller.

3. It allows you an extra few seconds to think through the answer and formulate your thoughts to stay in control.

Another idea:

When responding to the caller's questions, you may wish to include at least one of these phrases:

A. "Jim, here's a 3-step approach to help you decide what you want to do. You may find it helpful to write these 3 steps down."

B. "Sally, your situation is similar to Linda S. on Page 101 of my book. You'll find her case history helpful to you also. Let me tell you about her experience. She went from a $28,000 per year school teacher's position to a $75,000 per year job with a large national firm. Here's how she did it . . ."

Other Tips

Time Zones

In the continental U.S. there are 4 time zones (excluding Hawaii and Alaska). Internet Search Engines have an "Image" page where you can download or copy a time zone map of the US. Be sure to mark it "+1","-2" etc., so that you are always clear of the time you will be on the air.

*It's imperative that you take time out **before** going on the air to review the Radio Talk Show Confirmation Sheet.*

1. Highlight the name of the host.

2. Repeat the call letters of the station several times to yourself.

3. Make certain that you have the name of the program clearly in mind (and use the name of the program in your conversation with the host and listeners).

4. Also highlight the city and the state. People love it when you use these points of reference in your show. "It's a pleasure to be with you, Jane Show Host, and to be able to talk with your listeners in Kalamazoo."

I never turn my computer off. Before going on the air, I go to www.maps.google.com to the state where my show originates. I study the map and jot down the names of the surrounding towns, especially the name of the county in which the station is located.

Mentioning the names of the cities and county lets the host and listeners know that **you care.**

I learned the hard way that it's not always best to rely on my memory alone. One of the earliest shows I was on originated in South Bend, Wisconsin. My memory told me that South Bend (the one that I knew of) is in Indiana. Only after mentioning Indiana twice did the host politely correct me by saying, "We're in Wisconsin."

That was the last time that I relied strictly on my memory.

To make your show appearance a memorable one, let's talk about how you can

Leave Your Listeners With Something of Value!

Chapter 14

Leaving Your Listeners With Something of Value

Here's a tip on how to turn every talk show guest appearance into a **successful** talk show guest appearance.

During the first two months of being a guest on Radio Talk Shows I found myself reaching a plateau. I was getting results, but *not* GREAT RESULTS. I decided it was time to do some homework or research.

I kept my radios at home and in my car tuned to talk shows all the time. Talk shows became my most consuming passion. You know how it is when you are IN LOVE?

You can't think of anything or anyone else. Well, that's where I was at that time . . . **in love with radio talk shows.**

I listened to hundreds of guests on hundreds of programs. Many of them were good. Some of them were not so good. But they all had a common thread. They were all **alive and in love** with their topic.

Then one day . . .

I heard a guest who was not only in love with his topic, but who **loved it with a passion.** He wanted to make sure that his audiences got the most out of his talk. He left me with a **key** that turned my talk show experiences from good to **great.**

Every talk show after that became an extraordinary one. Every show became better than the previous ones. Every talk show now has a plan, a purpose and was achieving outstanding results.

The Key?

Get the Listeners Involved!

★ ★ ★ ★ ★

Getting listeners to go online and order your book

I decided that regardless of the length of the show (fifteen minutes, thirty minutes, or a full hour), I would always promise my listeners that they would receive three things from me by staying tuned to the program and station I was on.

Here's my promise to my listeners:

1. Tips on deciding what they want to do occupationally
2. New ideas on marketing oneself in a nontraditional but very positive manner
3. Three steps I guarantee will turn every interview into a Job Offer

You might be asking, "How can you squeeze all that into a 15-minute talk show?" It's easy. I just keep in mind that my audience of listeners is the most important reason that I am on the show.

Each of these three keys can be covered in two-to-three minutes (if need be). I can also expand each one into 10-to-15 minutes if time allows.

The expanded version includes additional examples, stories and incidents from seminars that I've conducted.

Listeners love to hear success stories. They want to know that others have done the same thing, and that they can do it too.

Nothing succeeds like Success. It's true. Sprinkle your interviews with success stories - stories about younger people and older people, stories about Easterners and Westerners, from the North and from the South. People all over America are alike. They want to succeed.

I attended the national convention of the National Speakers Association in Chicago. I sat near the front of the room at the closing banquet to hear Bob Richards. (For you younger folks Bob was the decathlon champion in the 1952 Olympics, and also the 'Wheaties man on TV' in the 1950s.) He left me with a 4-step formula that has proven successful in all of my talks.

Bob's formula?
1. **You can do it!**
2. **Don't give up!**
3. **In America your dreams can come true!**
4. **God will help you!**

You can't fault success. Bob Richards has given over 14,000 talks across America in the past four decades. He's used this formula every time. So if this formula works for Bob, **why not for you and me?**

Keep learning from every one of your experiences. You, too, will grow into the success that you want to be.

Now that my show format was getting better I wanted to make certain that listeners were able to contact me to order my book.

Here are more ideas on getting greater response to each of your radio talk shows:

Key #1 is to get listeners involved. Not only do you want them involved in listening to you, but also you want to give them a reason to stay tuned and to call in (if this is a call-in type show). Challenge them by making commitments and promises that you, of course, can fulfill. For example, on the front end of the program I tell the radio talk show host that I've created a **new** way to get jobs and GET EMPLOYERS CALLING APPLICANTS . . . and all this without resumes. I tell my listeners that resumes are left over from the 1970s. I then give them my favorite quote:

"If you do what you've always done . . .
you'll get what you've always gotten.
Is that enough?"

Think about this: If resumes worked, wouldn't everyone in America have a job?

So, let's do something different. That something different is the GOLD FORM that is highlighted in my book. Of course, this gives the host a perfect lead in to asking, "What is the Gold Form?" and "How did it come about?" etc.

Key #2 to getting listeners involved is to promise them something that they can use **right now!**

For example, about half way through the show I listen for the host to announce a break for commercials. I then jump in with: "When we come back, let's ask my listeners to get pencil and paper.

I've got a 3-step formula I guarantee will turn every job interview into a job offer."

Let me ask you. Who could say **no** to that question. Are any listeners going to turn to another program?

When I come back from the break, I remind listeners to get pencil and paper to write down the 3-step formula to turn every job interview into a job offer.

This is not a gimmick! This 3-step formula is part of the nuts and bolts in my book, *How to Get the Job You Really Want and Get Employers to Call You.* This 3-step formula (to the best of my research) has not been talked about or written about in ANY book on career change. Plus, following up on the students in my seminars proves that this 3-step idea works, and **gets people job offers.**

> *I proudly keep a letter I received from a listener from Garden Grove, California. She wrote me that the only part of my talk show interview that she heard was the 3-step formula to help a person turn a job interview into a JOB OFFER. She said that she was on her way to an interview and thought, "What have I got to lose . . . I'll try Joe's ideas." She closed her letter with, "Joe, I amazed myself. I used the 3 steps you gave me on the air, and GOT THE JOB! P.S. Please send me your book. I want to read about the rest of your system."*

Of course, when these listeners have written down the 3-step formula, they still have the pencil and paper in their hands. So that when I give out my website to order the book, they are ready and don't need to hunt for paper and pencil.

Key #3 is to make sure that the host AND the producer AND the switchboard of the radio station all have your website ahead of time. You'd be surprised how many people call the station long after the program is over asking: "How can I reach Joe who was on your station last week . . . last month?"

A one-minute call to the station's switchboard can produce extra orders. Ask the receptionist if you can leave your website with her in case listeners call the station after you are off the air.

I get orders weeks and months after the show is over.

Study these keys. Use these tips. They work for me. They can work for you, too.

Have listeners get paper and pencil so they can write down:

1. **Their perfect want ad idea.**
2. **Three keys to turn every job interview into a job offer.**
3. **The website to order your book.**

Chapter 15

Order Fulfillment and Streamlining Your Mail Room Procedures

How long should it take for you to fill orders for your book, CD or DVD?

Today I use the U.S. Postal Service to ship all my orders via Priority Mail that takes two days between major cities, and three days between all others. At the printing of this book, it is still just over $5.00.

What's surprising is the number of people who request Federal Express or similar overnight service. I guess we are into a Do It Now World, aren't we?

Here's another area where I discovered that time **really** is money.

My book orders come in spurts. Every time I do a talk show 95% of the orders come in via my email the same day. These orders are all credit card orders of course.

I always want to be able to fill and mail out these orders the SAME DAY they are received (as I promise on the radio). To keep me in a position to do this, I always have a stock of books ready to mail.

Here is how I handle my operation:

Once a day I pull up all of the orders that have been emailed to me. I put them onto my database program and print out personalized invoice/receipts and mailing labels for each order.

I then have one of my Assistants package up the products and send them out.

I once hired my neighbor, Mark, to work as my part-time mail person.

He was an 18-year old who was in his last year of high school. Every day after school (about 3:30 PM) Mark checked in "to see if there was anything I wanted done."

As a business major, Mark was fascinated by the mail order aspect of my business. He was receiving a practical education in business while I was getting responsible part-time help at a reasonable cost.

Mark did whatever it took to get the job done: collating, stuffing, sealing, stamping and labeling. With this process I was always several days ahead in the book readiness department. So when the orders came in, I only had to apply the labels and drop them in the last mail pickup (which is 5:30 PM near my home office).

Anticipating a run of talk shows is always a good idea. Make sure that your supply of books and materials is always far enough ahead to cover the needs for the next three or four weeks (or whatever length of time it takes you to reorder).

Here's another idea to make this project **fun**.

Keep a tally on the wall of your 'mail room' of the number of orders you receive each day. A simple chart with the date, and the number of credit card orders and mail orders and a total should do it. By keeping this tally sheet up to date you'll know how many books you have mailed out each day, and also 'month-to-date' and 'year-to-date.'

It's always fun to try to "beat last month."

Make sure you include rewards or prizes (even an ice cream cone). Remember you don't have a boss - unless you look in the mirror.

Challenge yourself.

Create a contest for yourself!

Make it fun . . . because it is.

Chapter 16

Getting Invited Back On the Same Show Again and Again

Here's how to get repeat bookings.

Anyone can get a radio talk show booking one time.

The real secret or key to success is being invited back again and again. Here's how to get that happening in your life.

First, you want to be **so good** that you will automatically be invited back. Second, structure your presentation so that you are planting seeds that will sprout in the near future.

Seeds? Yes, like: "I'm sorry we're running out of time. I have so much more to talk about that could help your listeners on KXYZ. I hope we can get together again soon to discuss _____ and _____."

Plus, follow up every program with a handwritten Thank You note or Appreciation-Gram.

People never forget folks who remember to say Please and Thank You. Most of us were taught these two words and phrases by our parents, but sometimes I think that "we are all grown up" now. We don't need to use them anymore.

73

If you want to be different, be different in a positive way. **Always** remember to say Please and Thank You. Better yet, always do it in writing **(handwritten preferred).** You will not only be remembered but be asked to return again and again.

I've been on several stations four or five times and plan to become permanent fixtures.

You can be, too.

This is a sample of the Appreciation-Gram that I use in my correspondence with Radio Talk shows.

Appreciation-Gram

(Actual size of this card is 5.5 x 4.25.
Use this area to write a personal note)

Joe Sabah • 303-722-7200 • Joe@JoeSabah.com

Joe Sabah   Postcard
PO Box 101330   Postage
Denver, CO 80210

A Special Note from Joe Sabah
Co-Author of Best Seller
How to Get the Job You Really Want
    and Get Employers to Call You
Author of results-getting book: Producer
    How to Get on Radio Talk Shows   Radio Station
    All Across America Without   Address
    Leaving Your Home or Office   City, State, Zip

Chapter 17

More Stuff That Works!

How do you keep going when things are not 'coming up roses'?

Above my desk I keep cards and letters from folks whose lives have been changed by ordering my book.

For example: Delores and Don of Bothel, Washington wrote me that by using the ideas in the JOBS BOOK they have generated four jobs: two for Delores, one for Don and one for a friend of theirs. In a card that came right before Christmas, they wrote: "God bless you for all the help you gave us when we were down and out."

Another letter from Albany, New York invites me to come to Albany and conduct a seminar in person. The writer of this letter is offering to sponsor the seminar and fill the seats with people.

Then there is the Mickey Mouse letter from Doug. (Actually written on Mickey Mouse stationery and mailed from Orlando Florida).

After being a guest for the second time on a Chicago, Illinois station, I received a request from a mother in Flossmoor (near Chicago) to send the book to her son who was in his junior year in college. Doug was interested in a summer job.

I'm delighted every time I read his letter.

"Dear Joe,

Thanks to you I was one of only two persons selected from my college campus to be invited to 'work' at Disney World in Orlando, Florida this summer.

Over 300 persons applied for these two jobs. I knew then that I would have to do something different to stand out from the crowd. The 'something different' I used was the idea in your book, *How to Get the Job You REALLY Want and Get Employers to Call You.* I created my own 'gold form' and used that instead of a resume. It worked. I got the job I wanted for the summer.

Doug

P.S. When I graduate you can be sure that I will use the 'gold form' idea again to get a permanent job. Thanks again."

Good Stuff!

★ ★ ★ ★ ★

Even Talk Show Hosts Use the Gold Form With Success

I was invited to be a guest on an Illinois radio station for the second time. The host was as cordial as he was the first time. As I was finishing up the show, the host asked, "Joe, would you stay on the line after we're off the air?" I said, "Of course."

He concluded his program. Then off the air he told me, "Joe, this is the last time that we'll be together on this station." I asked him to elaborate further. He exclaimed, "The Gold Form works!"

Still puzzled, I asked him to explain.

"I used the Gold Form and got another job, this time with a much larger radio station. In fact, it's with a satellite network."

I'm sorry to lose Tom as a talk show host for his former station, but he has sent me a copy of his Gold Form, and his new affiliation.

Next step: Another contact for a talk show on a Satellite network.

What to Talk About During Commercial Breaks

One of the most interesting interludes I experienced was during a commercial break on a major 50,000 watt station.

My favorite question to hosts is, "How did you get into radio?"

My host, Jim, excitedly told me about his varied background of selling, hotel management, etc. and confided, "I didn't have any radio background until I came to this station."

"But," he went on, "when I was seven years old I used to set up the card table in my family room. I'd drape a blanket over the table. Then I'd sit underneath my makeshift 'studio' and spin 45 rpm records on my little record player. So I guess you'd have to say that I've ALWAYS had a dream to be in radio."

So here I am – over 30 years later . . . **Living My Dream!"**

★ ★ ★ ★ ★

**Congratulations and best wishes to you as you
Live Your Dream and
Get on Radio Talk Shows All Across America**

I have one request of you: when you are booked on a Radio Talk Show in the Denver/Boulder area, please call me at 303-722-7200 or email me at Joe@JoeSabah.com

I will not critique you. I simply want to hear your passion and possibly call in to the show.

"Stay Well"

Joe Sabah

It's not always easy to get or keep inspiration. How do you do it?

If you could browse through my bookshelves here are some of the titles that have served me well:

The Bible

The Power of Positive Thinking, Dr. Norman Vincent Peale

How to Win Friends and Influence People, Dale Carnegie

How to Stop Worrying and Start Living, Dale Carnegie

The Fine Art of Doing Better, edited by D. John Hammond

How to Master the Art of Selling, Tom Hopkins

A Kick In the Seat of the Pants, Roger von Oech, PhD

A Whack On the Side of the Head, Roger von Oech, PhD

The Greatest Salesman in the World, Og Mandino

The Greatest Secret in the World, Og Mandino

The Greatest Success in the World, Og Mandino

The University of Success, Og Mandino

Human Engineering and Motivation, Cavett Robert

Move Ahead With Possibility Thinking, Dr. Robert Schuller

The Total Power of One in America, Fred Holden

Your Right to Fly, Dr. James Melton

Vital Enthusiasm, Dr. James Melton

The 7 Laws of Money, Michael Phillips

Jonathan Livingston Seagull, Richard Bach

Success Through a Positive Mental Attitude, W. Clement Stone

Conscious Happiness, Samm Sinclair Baker

Don't Talk About It - Do It!, Grant Gard

See You At the Top, Zig Ziglar

www.ingramcontent.com/pod-product-compliance
Lightning Source LLC
Chambersburg PA
CBHW081553220326
41598CB00036B/6657